A TALE OF TWO MALES

Poems by Wayne Courtois

Spartan
Press

Spartan Press

Kansas City, Missouri
spartanpress.com

Spartan Press

"As much as *A Tale of Two Males* points out the atrocities the gay community has endured with references to killer Bob Berdella, the assassination of Harvey Milk, and the torture and death of Matthew Shepard as well as those regularly bullied or beaten simply because they were gay, this book is a love story of how two men fought against life's challenges, found each other, and have a marriage that has endured over thirty years. Despite coming from two different countries where they have shouldered "pain/like a knapsack you will/never see into," they manage, "turning in [their] separate spirals" to find each other and enjoy life's simple pleasures like blowing bubbles, eating key lime pie in bed, or having a good cuddle. Courtois balances the dark times of youth with gentle moments of living with the love and light of your life. He says, "Let it be, let us be/unafraid to love each other.""

-Maryfrances Wagner, 6th Missouri Poet Laureate

"In *A Tale of Two Males*, Wayne Courtois offers a luminous, deeply human collection that is part love letter, part survivor's hymn, and wholly unforgettable. With gentle wit, brutal honesty, and aching tenderness, Courtois captures the everyday rituals, shared histories, and quiet intimacies of a long-term queer relationship— while never flinching from the political, cultural, and historical violences that haunt its margins. These poems chronicle not just a marriage, but a world: one shaped by resilience, memory, and the fierce insistence that love— real love—is worth recording. *A Tale of Two Males* will stay with you, not for its grand pronouncements, but for the warmth of its voice, the truth in its observations, and the reverent way it makes the ordinary shimmer."

-Rick Christiansen, author, *Not a Hero*

"*A Tale of Two Males,* the latest collection from Wayne Courtois, could well be one of the most nuanced, profound, and unflinchingly true love stories ever put to paper. Courtois's devotion not only to his soulmate, but also to his community and his craft are well in evidence throughout this groundbreaking collection. Courtois does what any good poet does: gives voice to the sublime hiding in the mundane, with such effortless skill that the reader is often left mid-poem pondering the many ways in which we all can find ourselves questioning, "Does God dance/on the head of the pin/we call now?" Time is a frequent visitor (though not always welcomed) in these poems. That will happen when one has lived a life of struggle and danger, a life often lacking the acceptance every one of us requires. But sprouting from those years of strife we see a perpetually flowering relationship to be admired for generations. Nothing is off the table, no topic is shied away from in this remarkable book. From the violence of a bigoted world to the annoyance of a noisy cat toy to the pains of aging to the ever-present fear of loss, Courtois draws us into his world, helps us acknowledge the brutality, and revel in the beauty. Indeed, "it takes/ lifetimes to make a lifetime," and we are all lucky the poet is sharing his with us. Throughout this admirable book of poems, between the lines of pain and struggle and regret, the strongest message prevails: "love endures."

-James Benger, author, *One Week*

Acknowledgments:

"First Date" first appeared, under a different title, in *Hibernation: Gay Poems from Gay Bards.*

"Coriolis" first appeared in *Gimme Your Lunch Money: Heartland Poets Speak Out Against Bullies.*

"Everything Old Is New Again" first appeared in *Chelsea Station.*

"The Lights of Cozumel" first appeared in *I-70 Review.*

Special Thanks to Jason Ryberg, Maryfrances Wagner, James Benger, Al Ortolani, Rick C. Christiansen, Catherine Anderson and Joel Barrett.

Table of Contents:

For Ralph, always

*"The longer I live, the more deeply I learn that love —
whether we call it friendship or family or romance — is the
work of mirroring and magnifying each other's light."*

- James Baldwin

Making Time

It takes a year to make a year.
Nothing brilliant here.

But how many nights can it
take to make one night, how

many mornings one morning?
I wait for light to creep
under the door, seep into

the carpet, always taking
its time. We're forever
between "last" and "next," and all

I have in this wicked space
is you. If I lost you, you'd
take everything. Time itself

would die. Yes, it takes
lifetimes to make a lifetime,
forevers to make forever.

We have eternity, you
and I, if only we can
make it happen *now*.

First Date

Two bulky men on a
winter sidewalk, taking leave
of each other, the night so

cold they kept their hands in their
pockets. The words they might have
said were only clouds of

vapor, the kiss they might have
shared in that public spot so
unthinkable, even the

stars were laughing. Two men
facing each other, that was
all. Yet here we are, many

years later, still facing each
other, remembering that
first goodnight.

Almost Nothing

I.

When you first saw me,
you saw almost nothing.

Flash of mustache,
speck of blue eye. Some guy.

Your glance barely
caught, and then—

what was that? More
than a surface? A bit of heart,

smidgen of gristle, scrap of light
from a star that died eons ago?

We are so slight—made of eternal
stuff, yet barely enough to last a lifetime.

II.

When I saw you,
I saw almost nothing.

Too focused on the room,
the past—that poor place—

the future, and the present
imperfect. What others thought,

if they thought at all.
You might have slipped away,

leaving me none the wiser.
Hard to picture today,

bound together as we are.
That first time—Did we speak?

Nod? Shake hands like straight boys,
strong grips soon forgotten?

When we walked, did I
lag behind, as I tend to do?

Or did we match our steps,
afraid not to? It was cold,

January weather.
I wasn't glib enough to say,

"We're not in these skins
forever." I knew so little,

not enough to measure. Now,
when my spirit feels small,

a chill passing quickly, like
a draft from a door already shut—

I recall that night when things
might have gone otherwise.

Was it chance?
Randomness catching our eyes?

Or was there
something more? Does God dance

on the head of the pin
we call now?

Coriolis

Fifty years ago, swept up in a life
I tried to care for—rules stringent,
pleasures few—I didn't, as the
song says, know about you. I lived
in the hardscrabble North, while

you lived down the crooked road,
in the bloody Southern Hemisphere,
where water swirled down the drain
clockwise. I couldn't help when
you were bullied and so alone.

Nor was I with you at the theater
in Quito where an old Mexican
horror film scared you to pieces. With
your older brother glued to the screen,
you took refuge beyond the back

row, hiding behind a musty curtain.
You parted it enough to peek now
and then through thick glasses,
nervous left hand smoothing a
cowlick as the black-and-white

nightmare drained the blood from your
face. It was the catacombs, and the
bones had come to life, shrieking

in terror. Even an infant stirred,
a hole in its skull crying for mama.

Scratches and static in the old film
added to the horror, as if it
wasn't meant to be seen. And
you made a choice. In the gloom
and dust of that theater, the

Spanish dialogue crackling in your
ears, you chose…not to. Not to
give in, not to horror. If you
had to hide, or look away, or
deny what was happening, you

would. You chose survival over
torment, the willingness to let
the curtain fall. Meanwhile, in
the Northern Hemisphere, where
water swirled down the drain

counterclockwise, I stood in
a six-foot snowdrift, waiting
for the school bus. Fat kid in
a parka, watch cap pulled over
my ears, snow blowing in my face.

I wasn't sure, when the bus
shouldered through the gloom, it
was really there, till it creaked and

sighed to a stop. I knocked my
numb feet against the door to clear

snow from my boots. My glasses
steamed up, snowflakes melted from
my eyebrows and eyelashes. The
bus lurched, I swung into a cold
plastic seat. How long till I could

feel my toes? One long ride past
many fields and a few houses
later, we reached the school. I
struggled down the path to the
gate, placing my boots in boot prints

that went before. I didn't expect to
stay upright for long. Sure enough,
a push from behind landed me in a
snowbank. Hands pulled my hood back,
shoveled snow down my neck. I'd

be wet and cold all day, my feet
thawing out, then freezing again
at recess. You could say I was numb
from the neck up as well. Eyes lowered,
voice squeaking, I never took the

practical path, choosing between
sanity and horror. My winter went
on forever, while you fought the good

fight, sweating out the days when
bullies had their ways and the

future looked grim. Perhaps we
were connected even then, tears
swirling down our faces in
different directions, meeting in
the middle. Turns out that swirling

thing is a myth—Coriolis doesn't
care about our personal drainage.
It has more important things to do,
far above our heads, like making
cyclones. Here's what matters:

turning in our separate spirals we
found each other, chose survival
over agony, and vanquished
the horror of our early years,
the difference in hemispheres.

Southmoreland Nights

Our first apartment together.

I.

Outside, below our bedroom window,
a scream. A tenant mugged.
Next day, I found Sam the maintenance guy
shaking his head at the blood on the concrete.
"Yeah," he said, "he whomped her good."

Sam had two semesters of
philosophy under his belt. One corner
of his smile turned up, the other down
as he let a few more words hang
between us in the chill autumn:

"She knew him."

II.

Footsteps in our parking lot
Near the tiny swimming pool.
Running steps. A man without a gun
chased by a shooter.
Pop. Pop. Like fireworks,
distant but approaching.

We dove for the lounge chairs.
Better not to have a pool
when you live next to a crack house.

III.

New Year's Eve, and at midnight
the neighbors across the street come out
on their porch, fire their guns, go
back in, come out with more guns
and fire those too. Turns out they've got
enough guns for several trips.

They say Kansas City
is the easternmost western town.

IV.

They weren't long, those Southmoreland nights,
and there would never be enough of them.
We lay in bed, holding each other,
too tired to speak,
our hands miming the words:

Baby, are you all right?
Are you all right, Baby?
It'll be all right, I promise.

Ad Astra

On the occasion of our wedding, October 18, 2013. One of the advantages of getting married after many years together is that you have lots of past history to draw from while writing your vows.

I reach for you
with arms of memory,
days and nights

slipping down
my fingertips.
I close my eyes,

feel the rain
that soaked us,
sun that baked us

on the coasts of Mexico.
The snowstorm in Maine
we drove through one night:

"Don't worry," I said.
"Visibility's fine."
I couldn't see a goddamn thing.

I reach for you
on the streets of New York,
the tundra near Estes Park,

The New Orleans guesthouse
where the bedsprings rang
like sleigh bells.

The room in Key West
where we ate key lime pie in bed
Like naughty boys.

The Kansas prairie where we
drove, lost, one summer night,
A miracle of stars above us.

I reach for you
in restless airports,
waiting rooms, funeral homes.

We got through the losses:
your parents, my mother and aunt,
as hard as we'd feared.

Meanwhile, picketers
and pundits likened us
to animals and pedophiles.

Two friends beaten
and left for dead,
one lost an eye, the other

his hearing in one ear.
Yes, they say we will suffer,
they say we are damned.

I see the first morning
I woke in your bed,
You in the doorway

Blowing through a plastic wand,
Filling the air with bubbles,
Each bearing a slippery rainbow.

We are the moments
That draw us close, like
The songs and poems,

Plays and movies
where we glimpse ourselves
and our hearts grow quiet.

Eternity is what it is,
The great divide.
Yet I reach for you,

And take your hand,
and feel the eternal
in us.

Everything Old Is New Again

A newlywed home: much to do.
And yet, nothing new. "I love you,"
and "Me too," like we used to.

Poking our thumbs east
and west: "He's my husband."
No disenfranchised jest.

We're serious. Got skin
in the game. A five-syllable
hyphenated name.

Things we've hoarded,
the dust and the riches,
gather round to gawk.

"Hey, bitches," they say,
"lookit you. On the right side
of history. Who knew?"

Nearby, at the rollercoaster,
the wrong-side-of-history folk
watch from below the steady tow

of our two-by-two cars up the hill.
Then we're gone, plunging
down, screaming, hearts lunging

in our throats. Oh,
wrong-siders, it's not just you.
We're strangers here too.

Now we steer
a hot-air balloon, up, up,
into the blinding afternoon.

Below, the wrong-siders
stare with bated breath. The pitch
of our basket augurs death….

We didn't know
history's right side was wild
and rocky like the sky.

But look, we're landing
without much fuss. it was only
ourselves we had to adjust.

Perhaps, when it all
shifts again, we'll put
our shoulders to it, too,

resisting change, the rude
pull of the future, like
a wound resisting sutures.

But the wrong-siders don't listen.
They watch the moonlight glisten
on the sea, as our tall ship

teeters toward the horizon line.
Well, fine. They still
think the earth is flat.

We'll slip over the edge,
they'll sigh with relief.
And that will be that.

Is It Safe to Say

Is it safe to say the world
will never see our love
again? As safe as it is

to say anything in these
mutinous times? We lowered
the flags to half-staff. The dead

nodded wisely. Most had died,
not because they were wicked,
but because they were hated.

Is it safe to say love is
stronger than lies? When we are
gone, will they lower the flags

to half-staff? Will they say we
died because we were hated?
We will look down, we will nod

wisely. Hate can kill,
but love lifts us higher.

Saturday Morning

Watering plants on our
tiny patio, how like
an angel you look in

sweatpants and T-shirt,
your thinning hair glowing.
Today we woke up, I felt

The back of your head, hair
flattened by sleep, ears alert,
and suddenly your face, lips

apart. One kiss. Another.
How can they taste the same,
always, as if we don't change?

A tender home we have, none
too clean, full of books and
papers, two cats denied

nothing. I see you bending
over their heads, I see the
things you love and I love them.

How do I know you won't die
And leave me alone?

How do I know you won't go,
Your body turned to ashes
As you wanted?

Nothing left of you but ash
Means nothing left of me.
How, how could you,
How could you do that?

Sometimes your smile is sad, as
if you, too, wonder if love
survives loss. I see you

watering plants, bending
over the small green shoots. I
see the things you love, and

I love you. This morning,
again, I shoulder my pain
like a knapsack you will

never see into. I step
out onto the patio.
"Good morning, my love."

And love endures.

I Thought We Agreed

During the night, the
cat found the toy with the bell.
I thought we had killed it.

During the day, the
toy with the bell hides well.
A bird it is, a soft canary,

with faux feathers, bell
tucked under its chin. And
it only comes out at night.

I thought we agreed: no toys
that ring, or squeak, or run on
batteries. Yet, in the middle

of the night, the bell.
As is often the case, you
have to remind me: the toy with the

bell was a Christmas present
from a friend we exchange gifts with,
including gifts for our cats.

I thought we agreed: no friends with
cats. They always give you things
for your cat that wake you up

in the middle of the night. This friend
lives in a house large enough to
accommodate toys with bells. But in

our condo, a bell that rings
in the living room
can be heard in the bedroom.

Even when you're snoring, and I'm
wearing earplugs. Husband, I
thought we agreed we wouldn't

always remind each other
of our forgetfulness, to
let our lapses in memory

lie undisturbed. Then there are
hard thoughts, hard truths that
also arise in the middle of the

night: somewhere not far from
here, perhaps in the next block,
we are hated. Someone is

sleepless with rage because we
exist, and have a marriage
and a house and a spoiled cat

with toys. If they could see us
pressed together in our
king-sized bed they'd hate us.

But we won't speak
of that, not in the middle
of the night when

I'm holding you tight and
breathing "I love you"
into your ear.

You, Part One

You are a different person.
Different from me,
different from others.

How do you manage this
without going insane?
You grew up

pouring orange juice
over breakfast cereal.
Yet your life

didn't go off the rails.
You eat French fries
with mayonnaise,

like Europeans do.
But the Statue of Liberty
let you in anyway.

You can fold a dinner
napkin into a striking
facsimile of a penis.

You can tie a cherry stem
into a knot using only
your tongue. What

happened? What clawed
you in the moonlight?
What bit you on the neck?

What mad scientist
brought you to life
with a lightning bolt?

You have loved me for years.
You still love me. You say
you will always love me.

My love, you are hopeless.

You, Part Two

You don't look like me.
Yet people think we're related.
"Yes," you'll say when they ask,

"we're related." Leaving it
there. Not getting into
"husband and husband,"

which is a bombshell
for many. Better let them
think we're the offspring

of first cousins, or something.
The other night, in bed,
my big toe crawled up

your leg, and I thought,
Is our skin made
of the same stuff?

How about our toenails?
"Ewww," you said, "Get
away from me with your

sharp nails." But that's just it.
I am away from you.
Does this need to be fixed

or let go, like a faucet that
drips but doesn't make noise?
Last night, during a storm,

you texted me: "Where are you?"
I texted back, "Nowhere.
Headed home."

What Endures?

Not much. Your voice,
your touch, your many
ways of smiling, the

way you tilt your head,
or snap the sheets
when you change the bed.

Your love of simple things,
your taste in wedding rings.
As for your taste in men—

what happened? Was there
only this shaggy face
at the husband store? You

could have done better, but don't
worry, dear. The one you love
is here. I like to think I

took you places you might not
have gone, showed you things you might
not have seen, the good and bad,

clean and unclean. If we've had
rough patches where our souls
collided, never were we

undecided. What endures? A home,
memories, companionship, and,
for me, knowing I'm yours.

When the Time Comes

When you were a child and your
door closed for the night, a small
light glowed in the corner of

your room. You closed your eyes and
told your heart you weren't alone.
Now, many years later, over

dinner in a restaurant
with other couples spaced
around us, we are quiet.

Wine glasses and tableware
speak for us. Other couples
look at us, look away. They

don't see that when the time comes,
and the sky burns red, and
mountains split open, and

darkness smothers us, I will
be your light. And we will tell
your heart you're not alone.

Yes, I sense how others see
us: quiet. They don't see the
swift current sweeping us

onward toward the light.

Hoarders

The herbs and spices
from 25 years ago
are no longer fresh.

They sit in their jars,
colors leached away.
They look like cigarette ash.

The teabags that expired
in 1992 are not at
their best. Sleepytime

will never wake up.
Red Zinger has zung.
And the canned goods

that have sat forever
have defied our parents'
bomb shelter dreams:

they won't last long
enough to bring the
future into harbor.

Looking around
for what will last,
I find you and me.

We've settled in,
bodies leaving sags
in the furniture,

loose hair in the bed.
Our minds have dulled,
balk at detail,

take us halfway upstairs,
where we stop. Wait, why
were we going upstairs?

And yet, day breaks
in the hallway window
where I see it each morning.

One day may come a flash:
the end of the world,
too quick to register.

We won't know for sure
what endures, until it
does. So far so good.

Sure They Do

As I sat down on my end
of the sofa, I knocked my
bowl of tortilla chips off

the end table, scattering
them on the carpet near and
far. I got down on my knees

to gather them up. I said
to you, on your end of the
sofa, "I hope these chips don't

get too fuzzy from the
carpet." Finished gathering,
I sat back down. You asked,

"Do you want some of my chips?"
"No, thanks," I said, scrolling through
the remote. "I'll eat these, as

soon as I find us something
to watch." You said, "What you should
do is blow on each chip

before you put it in your
mouth. That'll help with the fuzz."
I looked at the wall, blank like

me, and wondered: Do other
couples have these conversations?

Not Letting Go

On April 9th, 2013, Roger Gorley was beaten and arrested in a hospital room at Research Medical Center in Kansas City, Missouri, for refusing to leave the side of his inpatient husband, Allen Mansell.

The guards beat his wrists
to make him release the bedrail.
They slammed him to the floor,

scattering his glasses
and hearing aids, leaving
a smear of blood on the tile.

When the cops came, they put on
gloves. Universal precautions
before they handcuffed him.

They lie deep in the
queer subconscious, these
fears: fear of beatings,

fear of uniforms, fear
of lovers torn apart,
fear of loneliness,

and fear of the brokenness
they always say
will get us in the end.

What more than luck
has kept us safe so far?
Christ knows

there's precious little
of that. Oh, I could
let you go, but only

if fate took me, too,
saving me from a life
without you.

For now, I see them
always, the hands
clutching the bedrail,

white knuckles
in the half-dark of the
sickroom. And I write

down these words,
because writing them
feels like not letting go.

Photo Shoot

The reporter asked if we
could sit atop the wall.
Not without a forklift!

So we stood
with an arm around
each other's shoulders.

He fooled with the
camera. I thought these
things were simple now.

Had us stand close, closer.
Nearly on top of each other.
We didn't complain.

Had us turn at an angle.
you laced your fingers
to rest on my shoulder.

An unnatural pose
if ever there was one.
Maybe that was the point,

to show how natural
'unnatural' can be.
The pic looks great.

Noise in His Head

Ralph bends over the freezer
drawer, hunting a breakfast
burrito, his hair askew,

sweatpant cuffs brushing the floor.
Coffee should be brewing, but
he forgot to load the plastic cup in

the pot. And there's juice to pour,
a paper at the front door.
Heading there, he passes the

hall table with its unopened mail.
The skewed corners of number
ten envelopes call to him.

Bills, season tickets to renew,
special offers. It's all due
some attention, but look, in

the hall, Max has been scratching
in the box, there's litter on the floor.
It calls for a quick sweep,

while Jesus weeps at the burrito
defrosting on the counter, the
coffee unmade, the juice unpoured,

the paper in its plastic bag
by the door. Does that mail, by
any chance, have a note from

the accountant, something about
taxes, after two anxious days of
faxes? Into this scene

comes the husband—me—
trying to suss out
the breakfast status.

Ralph has been distracted
again, the noise in his head
whirring, obscuring

the order of the world, lives
lived logically, by lists of
things to be done, when and why.

I can't sort out his confusion,
but I can point, wiggle my
fingers, dance my eyebrows.

It's so easy to draw him
close, but few found that out
before me. Both of our

noisy heads settle down as
I stroke his brow, kiss his
hairline. My arm slides around

his shoulders and his eyes float
upward, hazel and serene.
Now the cat, having settled

in Ralph's breakfast chair, gets
unseated, shooed from the
table. I make coffee, loading

the tiny plastic cup
into the maker, not having
to see or handle the

actual product—this is
progress—and we begin the
togetherness of the day.

How often I'm surprised to
find I turned out this way.
Of all the men I've

known, I was least likely to
end up married. Yet we are both
the marrying kind, needing

this relationship as flour
and yeast need bread—something to
add up to despite the

occasional darkness in
our souls, the fear in our hearts,
or—yes—the noise in our heads.

A Haunted House

Four o'clock on a Saturday morning,
deep in a dream I won't recall. Into
the pitch dark of the bedroom comes
a sound: *beep...beep...beep....*

We're both awake, but I whisper, as
if not to disturb some third party:
"What is it?"

beep...beep...beep....

The first thing we think of is our
bedside alarm clocks.... easy enough
to tell they're silent. And the clock radios
in our bathrooms—Ralph has one, I have two,
one of them waterproof that I keep
in my shower...they are close to us as
well, closer than the *beep...beep...beep....*

Think, man, think! Is there anything in
our living room, filled with outdated media
like CDs and VHS tapes, that could be
making a beep?

The thermostat on the dining room wall?
The oven timer? The clock radio in
the kitchen? The timer that I use for my

red light therapy in the foyer?
What, oh what is that *beep...beep...beep?*

I swing my legs over the side of the bed and rise,
slowly. The beep...beep...beep is coming from
downstairs, that much is certain. I take the
carpeted stairs, not making a sound, not
even, it seems, breathing. *beep...beep...beep....*

The rest of the house is so still, as if
holding its breath...no, holding in a laugh,
because it's funny ha-ha that our electronics
have outwitted us, forcing me to creep around
like a barefooted thief, weirdly disoriented.
I wait till the house picks itself up, rotates one

turn and settles down again,
and I see I'm still in the living room.

Three steps take me to the dining room,
where yes, the *beep...beep...beep*
is louder, luring me into the kitchen.
Yes! It was the clock radio in the kitchen
all along, the one that we keep unplugged

because we've never been able to figure
out how the alarm works, trying to avoid
a nightmare like this, but see...you see,
the other day...all right, maybe it was
yesterday... I had plugged the beast in

so I could listen to the news while I
loaded the dishwasher. I pull the plug
which gives a less-than-satisfactory
reaction to my tug. Ha-ha, house, okay,
you got me good until next time.
I should be like the cat, who didn't stir
through all of this, who keeps her world
close to herself, closer than a sound
in the night that means nothing,

this night in the 21st-century, more
specifically the year Two-thousand Twenty,
a shit year if there ever was one.
Meanwhile you're missing me. What's
taking so long? Your whisper drifts down
stairs: "Hon? Hon?" Yes, I'm coming. Wait,
I need to say that out loud. "Yes, I'm coming.
And my feet are *freezing*."

A Winter's Bed

Find us in our winter bed,
far from the dreaded heat of
summer driving us to

opposite corners of the
sheets. Winter is sweet, sealing
us in a warm envelope,

cat curled at our feet. One night
I wake, filled with wonder, the
air chilled more than normal,

enough for my breath to show.
Beyond its steam I see, as
in a dream, your parents and

mine—our dead. At my side of
the bed my parents stand,
formal in posture, as if

waiting for a shutter to
click. Long-suffering New
Englanders, they seem more

confused than anything, as
startled by death as they had
been by life. My father, who

never knew I was gay—he
died before I knew myself—
turns his face away. "Jesus,"

he whispers, as he used to
do when he sat alone, always
alone, by the TV, and

a favorite team failed to
score. My mother just stares, a
corner of her mouth twitching.

I hardly know what to say,
but the words whisper themselves,
in clouds of breath: "What winter

hath joined together, let no
man put asunder." As my
parents fade, I see almost

too late they're holding hands. They
never did this. Chastely, like
sister and brother, they stand

as their lower bodies go,
then their joined hands, then their
torsos. Their faces, unchanged,

hover a moment, then flee.
I turn toward your side of
the bed to see your mother

leaning over you, smoothing
hair from your brow as the two
of you whisper in German.

Your father stands with his fists
on his hips, grinning half-
grudgingly at you, his

amused eyes saying, "Look at
this son we have made!
Whatever will we do with

him?" As they start to fade, you
reach out, your hand passes through
their ghostly forms. I hear a

sob as you withdraw, pull the
covers over your head. I
scoot over, fit my spoon-shape

to yours. What now? Before I
can find words, you're asleep,
pushing breath into your

pillow. The cat sneezes,
settles down again. Was that
all? And was it a dream? There's

no more time to wonder
before sleep takes me once more.
Now you and I are in

Heaven, another chilly-
outside, warm-inside place. Our
bed is the same, the cat.

Beyond generous windows,
sunlit clouds stretch forever.
Somehow I know they are

frosty to the touch. Angels
pluck slow, sweet music on the
icicles of their harps. My

cold nose rests on your shoulder,
cold toes on your leg. My cold
spots turn warm, again and

again. I whisper, "Do I
keep you warm?" You snuggle deep
into our spoon-shape. Are we

home for good, in this
eternal neighborhood? Where
are our dead? Will we see them

again? Such longing plagued our
lives on earth, but now.... Let the
wisdom find us, the questions

disperse like my breath on your
shoulder. What matters is what
has always mattered: we are

together, not alone. Can
forever last forever?
We will see.

Black-and-White

Black-and-White crossed our yard,
tail down, nose close to the ground,
several times a day coming around,
going where we didn't know, or what for,
or why it chose our yard, when
we hadn't done anything.

We ignored Black-and-White.
Who wouldn't pretend there was no such thing
disturbing the landscape, passing by
unbidden? Who wouldn't pretend,
and look the other way when
its head poked through the hedge?

Black-and-White, you've been gone now
for days, weeks. We pretended
we didn't see you. Now we can't see
anything else. Black-and-White,
how we cursed you,
how we looked away.

How we wish we had
another chance.

Live Jazz at the House of Pain

One morning years ago, your chronic back pain reached
the point where I first heard you say *"Ow"* as you came
  downstairs.
I was in the kitchen fixing breakfast. You were going
"Ow," on every step. I flattened myself against the
refrigerator. Was that really you? I peeked through
the kitchen doorway to see you seating yourself
at the dining room table, *"Ow, ow, ow"* as you lowered
yourself into the chair. I approached slowly, put a hand
on your shoulder, kissed the back of your neck.

Now whenever the pain strikes you go *"Ow!"*
I hate to hear it, but I understand. When your body
starts to betray you, speak up! Soon enough I've got
  my own go-to
gripe whenever my arthritic knee threatens to buckle.
It sounds like "Uh-*huh.*" We make a pair, loaded up
with groceries, heading between car and house:
"Ow." "Uh-*huh.*" *"Ow."* "Uh-*huh.*"

One night we're making up the bed, putting fresh
  sheets on,
even though it's after midnight, past our bedtime even
  on this Saturday.
On the radio is Coltrane's *A Love Supreme*, the live
Seattle recording from 1963 that sat on somebody's
  shelf until 2021—longer

than our time between changing sheets. To Coltrane
    we add our own
soundtrack: *"Ow."* "Uh-*huh.*" *"Ow."* "Uh-*huh.*"

Putting a fitted sheet on a king-size mattress is like
trying to put a condom on the Jolly Green Giant.
"Ow." "Uh-*huh*". Before I can say, "I need to sit
    down,"
I pitch forward, landing face-first on the blue-green
    expanse,
the color of sea and sky, perhaps the color of
    Coltrane's music.
"You okay?" "Just the knee, as usual." I struggle to
    sit up,
but a fitted corner snaps free, trapping my foot.

"It sounds fuzzy," you say. "The music."
"Well," I tell him, "it was a live performance at a
    club, and the record
was made from that. Then the record is played over
    the airwaves,
so we're what, three times removed…."
I recall a jazz critic referring to Coltrane's "sheets
    of music"—
flurries of notes like nothing heard before in his day.

"You sure know a lot about jazz," you say.
"No, I don't. It's like love, there's too much to know."

Without warning you cover me with the flat sheet.
A gentle reminder that I need to keep moving
if we're ever going to bed. I roll over, wrapping
    myself tight
in the flat sheet, bumping your thigh where you sit
    on the bed.
"This is a mess," I say, and you don't disagree, pushing

your thigh against me. *"Ow, ow, ow,"* you say, but softly.
I take the fetal position, my spine against your leg.
The music stops and I want to turn my mind off as
    well,
knowing I'll only have the usual luck. There is
too much,
way too much to know.

Two Cats

The tortoiseshell is the chatterer,
the worrier, like our mothers,
wondering why their sons
never took to the world
as other boys did—
pushing and shoving,
pitching and kicking,
poking it with a stick.
Jumping in feet first
while boys like us
stood aside, holding hands.
(Not really, but wanting to.)

Oh, little she-cat,
circling, worrying the space
around her missing womb...
Now comes the male, the ginger tabby,
leaping into view, pawing open
cupboards and drawers,
wanting everything.
I scoop him up, bury my face
in his coat.

Alternative Lives, Including This One

I am lying on the bed, but didn't tell you that's where
    I'd be.
Now I hear your footsteps without mine—footsteps
    that
don't know where I am or what I'm doing. They are
    the noises
you make on the squeaky floors of our house without
    me. As
if I were gone. What if I were gone? What would your
    footsteps
sound like, with no one else to hear them? Would they
    make
a sound at all? Or would my not-hearing-them make
    a sound?
Any sound at all?
Anything?

I found a cool new way of touching myself. Would like to
talk about this when you have a minute. You'd never guess
where I'm touching myself these days. I don't mean "where"
    as in the
library or the solarium, I mean "where" as on my body. You
remember my body, don't you? What a silly question, you
see the damn thing every day, or thereabouts!

I met the nicest boy. We kind of hung out together.
I felt safe with him, in a way I didn't feel safe
with other boys. Some of them would suddenly

do something like put a frog down my shirt,
or call me a name and run away, but XXX would
    never do that.
I thought maybe we would write to each other
after camp was over, but somehow we didn't, and
I don't know why. *All these crap years later and
I don't know why. All these dirty-jockstrap-in-my-mouth
years later and I don't know why. All these
too-big-and-shoved-up-my-butt-anyway years later.
All these jizz-soaked socks, all these cum-rag years later,
and how we used to laugh at "cum rags," and smiled
like we were cool, and like we secretly hated each other,
because that was how to be cool. The birth of
the cool, somebody called it, though they were talking about
jazz, not the putrescence of adolescence.*

Love Lies

Life's troubles announce themselves with noise.
This is especially true of men and boys.
They sound their warnings in advance:
Honey, you haven't got a chance.

Sometimes, with men and boys, you don't care.
There are joys attached, and you're willing to share.
Snatch defeat from the jaws of victory as you will,
for a while it's sweet, and very much worth the thrill.

I never looked for trouble, I looked for love.
Too bad love and trouble were hand-in-glove.
But while I knew that trouble came in many flavors,
elusive love granted me no favors.

You have to tease out love's presence, then
nurture it like a mama cat with a kitten.
They say trouble lies around every corner like
death, but it's love that lies, softly and sweetly—
a camouflaged trap, holding its breath.

Weekend Morning in Bed

Nothing graceful
in this nakedness,
nothing for the

Facebook wall,
the 24/7 media feed.
No one wants to see

my doughy flesh cascade
down your side
as I turn to hold you.

Nothing to see here, folks.
Yet I would stay here
rather than save the world.

Don't Have Enough

crap to eat
warmth for my feet

money for old age
words to fill a page

thoughts to fill my head
prayers for the dead

heart to last much longer
will to make it stronger

time to tell you
adequately
what your love means to me.

All My Love

because you keep me warm,
I love being warm-blooded.

because you are at my side
I love sleeping.

Because you sit across from me
I love eating.

(No, I would love eating
anyway.)

No love
matches my love for you.

You keep the world
turning, my heart beating,

the promise of heaven
in my soul.

The Lights of Cozumel

On the last night, we sit on the balcony,
breeze rubbing against us, warm and full.

White boats bob close to shore. Across the sea,
faint lights. "That must be Cozumel," you say.

I nod, as if I already knew. My restless mind
is at last night's cabaret, the drag queen's

Bacharach medley. *Forever and ever you'll be
in my heart, and I will love you forever and ever.*

Tomorrow, rehearsing fate, we leave. Nothing
lasts. A familiar gloom settles behind my eyes.

If I could pray, I would. *Save me from my thoughts,
save me from myself. This one time let it go.*

Between our chairs your hand finds mine,
fingers bumping, nuzzling each other like blind pups.

The oldest ritual we know. And just like that
the lights of Cozumel sharpen, grow perfect

in their distance. Nothing lasts. Yet forever must be.
We'll meet it halfway.

Stories of Us

I dreamed I was afraid of
oversleeping, yet couldn't
raise an eyelid to see if

dawn was peeping through the
louvered doors of the bedroom.
Sleep was solid as a tomb,

I was going nowhere. What
is there to wake up for?
Good God, can it really be

another day? You move, powning
your pillow, fisting it a good one.
I don't want to know what that means.

By the time the alarm rings
I've been awake a good hour,
sick of waking, as my fist

on the snooze button will tell
you. *Did you sleep okay? Me neither.*
I hope this not one of the

stories of us, getting up
in the morning, first kisses
with dry lips, where's the cat,

the socks I left by the bed,
the bathroom door? What's the dream
I had, and what does the

color of lavender have
to do with it...? Oh, I know,
it's the nightmare where I was

raped, and lavender was the
the color of my frock. That's
how I knew it was a dream,

I've never worn a frock
except at a couple of
costume parties. It's an old

dream, not a new one, a dream
I can think about without
freaking, just shaking my head

like I'm doing now. I look
around to see you sitting
on your edge of the bed with

one finger raised, the signal
you're going to sneeze, oh God!
Your sneezes never come

single file, but in a flock.
I take refuge behind my
bathroom door as you blast off,

one, two, three. Not bad, better
than coughs. You roused the
cat, she comes curling round my

bathroom door. Half-tabby,
half-white, she stays low, low,
low, her belly nearly touching

the carpet. Why is she always
scared in my bathroom? I'm the
one who should be scared, facing

my pale reflection like a
failed erection in the mirror
with its toothpaste spots.

One awkward turn and I'm
sinking, sinking onto the
toilet seat. My years of standing

at the bowl like a sturdy
oak are gone. Go, furry beast,
you've been creeping around here

long enough, go do what you
do, pleasure yourself on the
sofa. Husband, I should be

writing about our early
selves, the wild years, not the
pathetic souls we are now.

Or—I ask as an emptiness
rises in my gut—is there
anyone left to care?

The Dream Version

In the dream version, the Earth
is drowning and burning to death
at the same time. Always a miracle.

In the dream version, armies
look like ants storming the
same hills again and again,

expecting a different result
each time. In another type of
conflict, people are dying,

many with tubes down
their throats, others in an
agony of silence.

In the dream version
it comes down, as always,
to you and me.

We made a story.
We burned and drowned.
We stormed the same hills

again and again.
No one to notice, no one
To care. Is that why we did it?

In the dream version, we are
standing in the sun.
I hold you in my shadow.

When there is nothing left of
us the dream version lives on,
a floating memory without

form or substance, in the
universe of the unknown,
waiting for nothing.

Each Other

Thanksgiving 2013

I.

As we look out for each other—
like brother and brother,
only not—I think of my single

years, when I was a blot on
the landscape, clutching my hopes
like pennies—or pretending

to, when I hadn't any.
Me too, you say. Me too.
Yes, you had your own single

years, late nights in bars,
strangers in strange cars,
narrow escapes from disease

and death—we'll never know
how narrow. Back then, in
Kansas City, a psychopath

lured gay men to his midtown
home, tortured and killed them, and
garbage-bagged the body parts.[1]

When the story broke, the public
was aghast: "How horrible!" they
cried. "There are *homosexuals*

living here!" Now, fast forward
a double handful of years:
How have you and I spent our

hopes? The ropes of a relationship
take time to learn. But see,
among our flubs, the rub of

lovingkindness, willingness
to change and heal. Courtesy
comes with the deal: holding doors,

looking out for slippery
floors. Watch your step! This plate
is hot. Help me with my

coat, free a zipper, open
a jar? Will this fit in the
back of your car? Bring me

some water, some cherries,
some tea? My left ear is
bothering me. Yes, hon, I'll

eat the toast that's overdone.
Obsessed with each other much?
Still we keep in touch with

the news—gay couple attacked
by a mob in Philly, a
few days ago. Two trans

women injured, a gay man
shot dead in Detroit, another
beaten in San Diego.... I still

haven't learned to sew. I
love to watch you get your
sewing kit, sit on the edge

of the bed, choose thread, hold
my shirt gently, fastening
the button like a tiny

blessing. That soldier who was
beaten to death in his bed,
with a baseball bat?[2] He was

from around here...
Have you fed the cat?

II.

Oh, spilled coffee,
look at the mess I made. Yes,
sometimes I'm afraid. Many

hate us, spewing bile while we
do what we do, fold laundry,
fix a tile. What we hate is

that light fixture on the
second floor, the one we need
a stepladder for when a

bulb blows out. What scares me
most? Haters who get their hate
from some Holy Ghost. We'd

better get dressed, you know our
hosts. Did one of your socks go
missing? This one? Oh, look: a

crowded gay bar in Boston
threatened by a teen with
a hatchet and a gun. Two

lesbians attacked by ten
men in Austin. I know, I
say I won't read these things, yet

there I go. And other parts
of the world are so bad. That
young man in Volgograd[3] : raped

with beer bottles, genitals
slashed, skull crushed with a
stone. Where does the hate go

afterwards? Is it time for
a beer, or another queer?
Your keys are on the sill. My

pills are upstairs. Caught unawares,
most of them—the shot, stabbed,
beaten, hanged, burned, drowned.

Bodies left in trash cans, buried
in shallow graves. Suicidal
teens, too many to save—that

Rutgers student who jumped off
the George Washington Bridge[4]....
The wine is in the fridge.

Take an umbrella, looks like rain.
Can you kill the light?

III.

Outside, away from our nest,
the world expands in a way
it doesn't quite on the

Internet. How innocent,
these rows of silent homes. Who
hurls the first stone, who's the

sinner? Can't talk about this stuff
at dinner, Dustin and Craig
would have a fit. These houses

will wear Christmas lights soon....
Where does the sorrow go? Do
we rend our clothes? Curse God?

Sicken ourselves with grief? You
and I can't kick, we've had a
good year, you got freelance

work, I got something in print.
We won't stint on the cornbread
dressing or cranberry sauce.

Will it be pecan or
pumpkin pie? Both? You're the
boss. Soon enough we're gathered

at the groaning table,
trying as best we're able
to show holiday cheer. The

wine helps. Have another? Yes.
I've been sneezing a lot, just
getting a cold. And the aches

and pains, part of growing old.
Conversation lags. Dustin
and Craig argue over whether

or not Phillip Glass is a
fag. Look, Phillip Glass is one
of those celebs who should be

gay, but they're not. All right?
Coffee and pie. A toast.
Another. And another.

I feel like going away. Never
enough time for a trip. My lips
are numb when I tell our hosts

goodnight.

IV.

We get home all right.
I have a headache. I'll just
lie down. Can you kill the light?

The end of a long day, one
more Thanksgiving put away.
Tell me, I've never asked you

outright: Why are we here? No,
I don't mean just *living*. You
and me, do we mean anything?

We've seen the spaces of our
mutilated history—
San Francisco City Hall,[5]

the fence outside Laramie,[6]
the New Orleans streetcorner
where the Upstairs Lounge used to

be.[7] It's not the wine talking,
I feel it all the time, this
urgency drilling down to

the bone: Do even our lives
have meaning? Do you lean one
way or the other? Here is

all I know: tonight I saw
your eyes by candlelight. It
brought tears to my own. You

were my dream, before I dared
dream. Before I knew the
fear of having so much to

lose. No, it's not the wine
talking, as I take your hand
in mine. In every way

that counts, you *are* my brother.
Let it be, let us be
unafraid to love each other.

1. The killer was Bob Berdella. After one of his victims escaped, Berdella was caught, tried for six murders, and sentenced to two consecutive life sentences. He died in 1992, after four years in prison.

2. On July 6, 1999, PFC Barry Winchell was beaten to death where he slept by Calvin Glover and Justin Fisher at Ft. Campbell, KY. Winchell's "crime," in the eyes of his killers, was dating a transgender night club performer.

3 The 23-year-old was tortured to death by two men on May 10, 2013, after stating that he was gay. In time, Russian authorities made the rare admission that it appeared to be a hate crime.

4. In September of 2010, 18-year-old Tyler Clementi committed suicide by jumping off the George Washington Bridge. His Rutgers roommate had secretly recorded him while he was kissing another man and shared the video online.

5. Harvey Milk was assassinated by Dan White at San Francisco City Hall on November 27, 1978.

6. In October of 1998 Matthew Shepard was beaten, tortured, tied to a fence, and left to die in Laramie, Wyoming.

7. In the worst mass killing of gays in U.S. history, 32 men were burned to death in a fire at the Upstairs Lounge in New Orleans on June 24, 1973. (Tragically, this record would be broken on June 12, 2016, when 49 were murdered at The Pulse nightclub in Orlando.)

Wayne Courtois was born in Portland, Maine, and currently lives in Kansas City, Missouri with his husband, Ralph Seligman. In January 2026 they will celebrate 37 years together.

A graduate of the MFA Program at the University of North Carolina-Greensboro, Courtois is author of a memoir, *A Report from Winter;* a novel, *Tales My Body Told Me;* and two erotic novels, *My Name Is Rand* and *In the Time of Solution 9.* His short fiction and poetry have appeared in journals including *The Greensboro Review, Harrington Gay Men's Literary Quarterly, Assaracus, Jonathan,* and *The I-70 Review,* in the webzines *suspect thoughts: a journal of subversive writing* and *Velvet Mafia;* and in anthologies such as *The Shining Years, Gimme Your Lunch Money, Best Gay Erotica,* and *Hibernation and Other Poems* by Bear Bards. His nonfiction has appeared in *I Do/I Don't: Queers on Marriage; Walking Higher: Gay Men Write about the Deaths of Their Mothers;* and *The Lost Library: Gay Fiction Rediscovered.*

Courtois has served on the local Ryan White Planning Council, and as a grant writer in the nonprofit sector has helped to raise millions for HIV/AIDS services, hospice care, and the arts.

This project was made possible, in part, by generous support from the Osage Arts Community.

Osage Arts Community provides temporary time, space and support for the creation of new artistic works in a retreat format, serving creative people of all kinds — visual artists, composers, poets, fiction and nonfiction writers. Located on a 152-acre farm in an isolated rural mountainside setting in Central Missouri and bordered by ¾ of a mile of the Gasconade River, OAC provides residencies to those working alone, as well as welcoming collaborative teams, offering living space and workspace in a country environment to emerging and mid-career artists. For more information, visit us at www.osageac.org

Osage Arts Community